What the prof ✍ S0-BAY-509
about this manual:

Advice on how to quit smoking is easy to come by. This book, however, is considerably more than mere advice. It represents the results of many years of research on methods for successful quitting.

Patrick A. Boudewyns, Ph.D.
Professor, Department of Psychiatry and Health Behavior
Medical College of Georgia.

A remarkably clear, practical guide to assist those who want to stop smoking!

John R. Feussner, M.D.
Director, Region 2
Health Services Field Program
Veterans Administration

QuitSmart tells the smoker who wants to quit permanently exactly what he/she needs to know.

John F. Higdon, Ph.D.
Assistant Professor, Department of Psychiatry
School Of Medicine
University of Missouri-Columbia

The QuitSmart book and tape are terrific. It is the finest most useful tool I've ever seen to help smokers quit. I'm recommending it to all my patients who are smokers.

Belinda R. Novik, Ph.D.
Practicing Clinical Psychologist and Past President North Carolina Society of Clinical Hypnosis

QuitSmart stacks the deck strongly in the client's favor. ... The package is heartily endorsed by this reviewer.

Reid Whiteside, MA
North Carolina Society of Clinical Hypnosis Newsletter

QUIT SMART™

A GUIDE TO FREEDOM FROM CIGARETTES

Dr. Robert H. Shipley

JB PRESS
DURHAM, NORTH CAROLINA

JB Press, P.O. Box 4843, Duke Station, Durham, NC 27706
(For book ordering information, please turn to the last page.)

ISBN Number: 0-9614881-8-2 (1990 Manual)
                      0-9614881-9-0 (1990 Manual and
                          Self-Hypnosis Audiocassette)
Library of Congress Catalog Card Number: 86-80034

Printed in the United States of America

To the thousands of people who
allowed me to share their journey
to freedom from cigarettes.

Preface

Cigarette smoking is the major preventable cause of illness and death in the United States. Most smokers realize this and want to be free of cigarettes, but until recently, effective treatments to help them quit did not exist. During the past several years, effective treatment methods have been discovered. These treatments address both the addictive and psychological components of tobacco smoking as well as various side effects of quitting (such as anxiety and depression) that can undermine quitting efforts.

As Director of the Quit Smoking Clinic at Duke University Medical Center, I have observed first-hand the superior effectiveness of these treatment methods as they have helped thousands of people quit smoking. This manual presents these powerful treatments. It is designed to help people who want to quit on their own and also as a companion manual for people enrolled in formal quit smoking clinics.

I am a former smoker who went through considerable struggle before finally breaking free of cigarettes. I know that deciding to quit smoking is difficult. While the rational part of you knows you will be better off without cigarettes, another part of you probably enjoys smoking and does not want to give up that pleasure. One of your first tasks in working with this manual will be to resolve these mixed feelings.

This manual presents the most up-to-date, scientific, *smart* ways to quit smoking. By reading this manual and using the recommended procedures, you have a good chance to gain permanently your freedom from cigarettes! Good luck.

Robert H. Shipley, Ph.D.

Acknowledgments

I wish to thank Jennifer Shipley and Alice White for their loving support and encouragement.

Many thanks also for expert technical assistance and encouragement from Jane Peppler in design, layout, and typesetting, Jeanine Wheless in editing, Janet Shipley in manuscript preparation, Allen Feinberg in priority setting, Su Pickett of West Side Studio in cover design, and Chris OBrion in cartoon creation.

I am indebted to Alice White, Steve Herman, Jack Feussner, Jean Shipley, Kim Lawrence, Sam Dickey, Pat Lees, Louise Koslofsky, and Ed Watkins for thoughtful reviews of early drafts of this manual.

Contents

Preface...................................iv

Acknowledgments..........................vii

Introduction.............................10

I. **Preparing to Quit**...................12

The Memory Jogger.....................14

Why Cold Turkey Quitting?.............16

Are You Addicted to Nicotine?.........18

Brand Switching to Reduce Addiction.....20

Nicorette® (Nicotine Gum).............30

Should You Reduce Caffeine
  Consumption?........................32

Stop the Debate......................36

Enlist Allies........................37

Avoid Smoking Temptations............40

Make Cigarette Substitutes Available.....41

Select Your Quit Date................42

II. **Quitting**..........................44

Learning to Relax....................46

Thinking Makes It So.................49

Keeping Withdrawal Symptoms
  in Perspective......................52

Habit Buster Tips....................56

Coping Techniques to Remember........58

III. **Remaining a Nonsmoker** 60

Maintaining Your Emotional Balance. 62

Rebuffing Smoking Come-Ons 66

Controlling the Enemy Within. 68

Staying on the Wagon 70

Systematic Weight Control 72

Dangers of Smoking / Benefits of
    Nonsmoking 75

What Next? 82

Appendix: Self-Hypnosis 87

Introduction

Congratulations on your decision to adopt a healthier lifestyle by breaking free of cigarettes. Success in this endeavor, as in most areas of life, depends on "keeping your head" and using the best techniques available. This QuitSmart manual provides the information you need. As you read and reread it, you will be able to succeed with greater ease than you thought possible. Quitting is not so much a matter of *willpower* as it is of *skill*—doing the right things and thinking the right thoughts to guarantee success. In the sections that follow you will learn to:

- Keep your reasons for breaking free of cigarettes prominent in your mind.
- Ease nicotine withdrawal by systematic use of low-nicotine cigarettes prior to quitting, and nicotine-replacement gum after quitting.
- Use your thoughts to make quitting easier.
- Relax during the withdrawal phase with breathing techniques, proper nutrition, and exercise.
- Enlist the support and encouragement of others.
- Avoid weight gain.
- Maintain your emotional balance.
- Avoid smoking temptations and successfully deal with smoking "come-ons."
- Stay free of cigarettes for life.

To quit for good, read this manual and formulate your quitting plan; decide when you will quit, whether you will switch to cigarettes with less nicotine before quitting or use nicotine gum after quitting, and on which coping techniques you will rely.

There are three chapters in this manual, corresponding to phases of quitting: **Preparing To Quit**, **Quitting**, and **Remaining a Nonsmoker**. During each phase of quitting, study the chapter for that phase and for the subsequent phase. In this way, you will always be prepared with appropriate coping techniques. When preparing to quit, for example, you should study Chapter I, **Preparing To Quit**, and Chapter II, **Quitting**.

Refer often to this manual. It was kept small so that you can carry it with you. Read with pencil or pen ready because you will be an active participant in this learning experience. Practice the recommended coping techniques, even those that seem at first a bit silly or unnecessary. When you use the coping techniques presented in this manual, you will have a good chance of success.

Be proud of your decision to break the cigarette habit. You are already on your way to feeling better and to a healthier life!

QUIT SMART™

CHAPTER I:
Preparing to Quit

J ust as you plan for a trip by thinking ahead and deciding what you will need to take along, the sections in this chapter will help you plan ahead for successful quitting. First, you will be asked to enhance your quitting motivation by listing your reasons for wanting to quit smoking, and you will plan a method of cold-turkey quitting which matches your preferences and needs.

Next, by enlisting the help of people around you and by arranging your home and work settings to lessen temptation, you will obtain maximum support for your quitting efforts. Finally, you will select your quit date—your first day of freedom from cigarettes.

Prior to quitting, you will also want to read Chapter II, **Quitting**, so you will have effective coping techniques ready to use on your quit date. One procedure that many find helpful is self-hypnosis. A self-hypnosis tape is available for use with this manual. Consider sending for this tape now so you will have it on your quit date (see page 87 for more information).

The Memory Jogger

You have good reasons for quitting cigarettes, but did you know that most exsmokers soon forget why they quit in the first place?

Sharon quit smoking because she could not walk up the stairs without becoming short of breath, and she felt tired most of the time. Three months after quitting, she could run up the stairs and felt alert and energetic most of the time. However, she could no longer remember exactly why she had decided to quit smoking. She soon started smoking again.

The next time Sharon decided to quit smoking, as a reminder of her reasons for quitting, she put a list in her kitchen and above her desk at work. This time she was able to remain free of cigarettes. Try using a memory jogger. Make a list of your reasons for quitting; for more ideas, see pages 78-81. Display one copy of your list prominently at work and another copy at home.

I'm quitting cigarettes because:

_____

_____

_____

_____

_____

_____

_____

_____

_____

_____

_____

_____

_____

_____

_____

_____

_____

Why Cold Turkey Quitting?

Recent studies have shown that cold turkey quitting (quitting entirely on a selected quit date) results in more success than cut-down quitting (gradually cutting down the number of cigarettes smoked). In fact, cut-down quitting increases and prolongs withdrawal symptoms. Trying to quit gradually is like trying to end a love affair by gradually seeing the person less and less; perhaps it can be done, but it is very painful.

Cut-down methods increase the time of painful indecision about quitting, and teach the smoker to value cigarettes even more because each rationed cigarette is smoked when it is most desired. Cutting down fosters the illusion that one can quit smoking and yet still smoke some cigarettes (i.e., "have your cake and eat it too"). In trying to quit by cutting down gradually, a person typically has difficulty reducing beyond seven to ten cigarettes per day, and with the first crisis, resumes regular smoking. Perhaps you've had this experience in the past.

Quitting cold turkey is desirable because it forces a decision never to smoke again, because it limits withdrawal symptoms to a brief period of time, and because it is associated with a high rate of successful long-term abstinence. The one disadvantage of cold turkey quitting is that the sudden elimination of nicotine intake can be difficult for people who are physically addicted to nicotine.

The next section lets you determine if you are addicted to nicotine. If so, instructions are provided for two methods to wean your body gradually from nicotine. The first is by switching to brands of cigarettes with progressively less nicotine prior to quitting cold turkey, and the second is the use of nicotine-containing gum after cold-turkey quitting.

Severity of cigarette craving for those cutting down versus those quitting cold turkey.

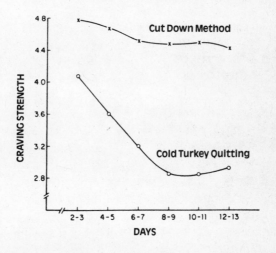

Adapted from S.M. Shiffman's "The Tobacco Withdrawal Syndrome." In N.A. Krasnegor (Ed.) *Cigarette Smoking as a Dependence Process* (Monograph 23). Rockville, MD: NIDA, U.S. DHEW, 1979.

Are You Addicted to Nicotine?

Many smokers are physically addicted to the nicotine in cigarettes. If they do not smoke for a time, the nicotine level in their blood drops and they experience a strong physical urge for a cigarette. Answer the questions below to see if you are physically dependent on the nicotine in your cigarettes.

1. Do you smoke more than 18 cigarettes a day?	yes no
2. Does your brand of cigarettes contain 0.6 milligrams of nicotine or more? (see Table in next section)	yes no
3. After you awake in the morning, do you smoke your first cigarette within 20 minutes?	yes no
4. Are you quite bothered or upset if you run out of cigarettes or find yourself in a place where you can't smoke for a few hours?	yes no

If you answered yes to three or four questions, you probably are addicted to nicotine. You can ease your physical withdrawal from nicotine by switching to brands of cigarettes with less nicotine before you quit cold turkey and/or by using the new prescription nicotine gum after you quit. These options are discussed in the next two sections of this manual. If you answered yes to two or fewer questions, you probably are not physically addicted to nicotine. You can quit cold turkey without brand switching or nicotine gum.

NOTE: *Do not attempt to quit cigarettes by switching to pipes, cigars, chewing tobacco, or snuff.* Use of each of these tobacco substances carries a substantial health risk. Use of chewing tobacco or snuff can cause gum disease and oral cancer. Pipe or cigar smoking may cause heart disease and lung cancer. Even those pipe or cigar smokers who believe they do not inhale the smoke are at risk. Research has shown that cigarette smokers who switch to pipe or cigar smoking unconsciously inhale significant quantities of smoke into their lungs.

Brand Switching to Reduce Addiction

If you are addicted to nicotine, quitting will be easier if you first reduce your physical dependence on nicotine. The best way of doing this is by switching each week to a brand of cigarettes containing less nicotine. To determine the nicotine content of your cigarettes, find your exact brand in the Table on the following pages. For example, if you smoke Kent Golden Light 100's, you are consuming 0.9 milligrams of nicotine in each cigarette (Box 9 in the Table). Other Kent brands have different amounts of nicotine, so it is important that you find your *exact brand* in the Table.

Within the box listing your cigarette brand are instructions to switch to a new box number. Select a brand from the new box and smoke it for one week, maintaining the number of cigarettes usually smoked. Then select a brand from the next indicated box and smoke it during the second week. Continue this way, switching to lower nicotine cigarettes each week, until you are smoking a brand in box 3; these brands have 0.3 milligrams of nicotine or less. This will take one to three weeks. If you are already smoking cigarettes with 0.3 milligrams of nicotine or less, you do not need to switch brands.

Example: Gerry smoked thirty Camel Filter Kings each day. She found this brand in box 10 of the Table (1.0 milligrams nicotine) and saw that she should switch to a brand in box 6 (0.6 milligrams nicotine). She selected Camel Light Kings and smoked thirty of these a day for one week. For the second week she switched to a brand in box 3 (with 0.3 milligrams nicotine). Then she quit cold turkey, and because 70 percent of the nicotine had already been eliminated from her body, she had very few physical withdrawal symptoms.

In smoking each low-nicotine brand, be careful not to defeat your purpose of taking in less nicotine. Smoke no more than your usual number of cigarettes and do not inhale more deeply or smoke the cigarette further down! Also, be careful not to cover the air ventilation holes placed around the filter of some low-nicotine cigarettes.

When following the brand-switching strategy, you probably will not enjoy the low-nicotine brands as much as your regular brand. This is helpful, since a less-enjoyable brand will be easier to give up when your quit day arrives. However, avoid the temptation to switch immediately to the brand lowest in nicotine; you would experience physical withdrawal symptoms and a lot of frustration with the new brand.

Write below the brands you select:

The first week I'll smoke

_____ (brand)

The second week I'll smoke

_____ (brand)

The third week I'll smoke

_____ (brand)

Determine if your cigarettes are Regular, King, 100s, or 120s by comparing them to the drawings below.

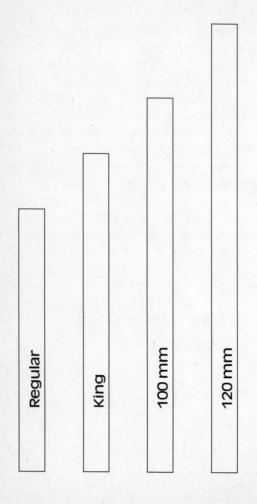

Regular   King   100 mm   120 mm

TABLE: Cigarettes Grouped by Nicotine Content

Instructions: Find your exact brand. Each week switch to a brand in the next specified box. Quit after you complete box 3. Brands are filtered (F), nonmenthol (NM), unless specified nonfilter (NF) or menthol (M). Private label store brands (e.g., Cost Cutter, P & Q) are listed as Generic.

Barclay and Kool Ultra brands are not listed because accurate nicotine values are not available. If you are smoking one of these brands, you should switch to a brand in box 3.

15

1.7-1.9 Milligrams Nicotine
Switch next to Box 10

Chesterfield–King (NF)
English Ovals–King (NF)
Generic–King (NF)
Old Gold Straights–King (NF)
Players–Regular (NF)
Pyramid–King (NF)

14

1.5-1.6 Milligrams Nicotine
Switch next to Box 10

Generic FF 100
Herbert Tareyton–King (NF)
Lucky Strike–Regular (NF)
Max 120 (M & NM)
Newport 100 (M)
Old Gold Filter 100
Pall Mall–King (NF)
Philip Morris Commander–King (NF)
Spring 100 (M)
Tall 120 (M & NM)

13

1.3-1.4 Milligrams Nicotine
Switch next to Box 9

Camel–Regular (NF)
Chesterfield–Regular (NF)
Class A Deluxe FF–King
Class A Deluxe FF 100
Dunhill International 100
Generic FF–King
Kool–Regular (NF, M)
L&M 30's Full Flavor 100
More 120 (M & NM)
Newport–King (M)
Old Gold Filters–King
Philip-Morris–Regular (NF)
Pyramid FF–King (M & NM)
Pyramid FF 100 (M & NM)
Raleigh–King (NF)
Richland 100 (M & NM)
Rothmans–King

12

1.2 Milligrams Nicotine
Switch next to Box 8

Benson & Hedges–King
Benson & Hedges 100 (M & NM)
Cambridge Full Flavor 100
Class A Deluxe Lights–King
Class A Deluxe Lights 100
Convoy–King
Dunhill Menthol 100 (M)
Generic–Regular (NF)
Generic Lights–King (M & NM)
Generic Lights 100 (M & NM)
Kool–King (M)
Lark 100
L&M Lights–King
Marlboro Red 100
Marlboro 100
Pall Mall 100

(continued on next page)

1.1 Milligrams Nicotine
continued from previous page

12

Philip Morris Blues–King (M)
Philip Morris 100 (M)
Philip Morris International (M & NM)
Picayune–Regular (NF)
Richland–King (M & NM)
Salem–King (M)
Salem 100 (M)
Stride Deluxe Lights–King (M & NM)
Stride Deluxe Lights 100 (M & NM)

1.1 Milligrams Nicotine
Switch next to Box 6

11

Alpine–King (M)
Cambridge Full Flavor–King
Camel Filters 100
Century 25's 100
Craven "A"–Regular
Craven "A"–King
Doral Full Flavor–King (M & NM)
Doral Full Flavor 100 (M & NM)
Eli Cutter–King
Eve Lights 120 (M & NM)
L&M Super Lights 100
L&M 30's Lights 100
Lark–King
Lark Light 100
Marlboro–King (M & NM)
Pall Mall Light 100 Low Tar (M)
Pall Mall Unfiltered Lights–King (NF)
Pyramid Lights 100 (M & NM)
Saratoga 120 (M & NM)
Savvy Lights 100 (M & NM)
St. Moritz 100 (M & NM)
Viceroy Super Long 100
Virginia Slims 100 (M & NM)
Winston–King
Winston 100

10

1.0 Milligrams Nicotine
Switch next to Box 6

Camel Filters–King
Eve Slim Lights 100 (M & NM)
Hi–Lite 100
Kent 100 (M & NM)
Lark Lights–King
Lucky Strike 100 (M & NM)
Malibu 100 (M & NM)
Newport Lights 100 (M)
Newport Stripes 100 (M & NM)
Old Gold Lights 100
Pall Mall Red–King
Pall Mall Red 100
Parliament Light 100
Players 100 (M & NM)
Pyramid Lights–King
Raleigh–King
Raleigh 100
Rothmans Special Mild–King
Satin 100 (M & NM)
Silva Thins 100 (M & NM)
Tareyton–King
Tareyton 100
Viceroy–King
Virginia Slims Lights 120 (M & NM)

9

0.9 Milligrams Nicotine
Switch next to Box 5

Benson and Hedges Multifilter–King
Cambridge Lights 100 (M & NM)
Century 25's–King
Chelsea–King (M & NM)
Eli Cutter Lights–King
Falcon Lights 100 (M & NM)
Kent–King
Kent Golden Lights 100 (M & NM)
Kim 25's 100 (M & NM)

(continued on next page)

9

0.9 Milligrams Nicotine
continued from previous page

Kool Milds–King (M)
Kool Milds 100 (M)
Lucky Strike–King
Magna–King
More Lights 120 (M & NM)
Old Gold Lights–King
Raleigh Lights–King
Raleigh Lights 100
Richland Lights 100
Silva Thins 100 (NM)
Viceroy Lights–King
Viceroy Lights 100

8

0.8 Milligrams Nicotine
Switch next to Box 5

Belair–King (M)
Benson and Hedges Lights 100 (M & NM)
Cambridge Lights–King (M & NM)
Camel Lights 100
Capri 100 (M & NM)
Century 25's Lights 100 (M & NM)
Dunhill International Superior Mild 100
Falcon Lights–King (M & NM)
Kent Golden Lights–King (M & NM)
L&M Long Lights 100
Lucky Strike Lights 100
Marlboro Lights–King (M & NM)
Marlboro Lights 100 (M & NM)
Merit 100 (M & NM)
Pall Mall Lights 100
Players–King (M & NM)
Players Lights 25's 100 (M & NM)
Richland Lights–King
Ritz 100 (M & NM)
Salem Lights 100 (M)
Salem Slim Lights 100 (M)
Vantage Excel 100
Winston Lights 100

7

0.7 Milligrams Nicotine
Switch next to Box 4

Belair 100 (M)
Century 25's Lights–King
Class A Deluxe Ultra Light–King
Class A Deluxe Ultra Light 100
Doral Filter Lights–King (M & NM)
Doral Filter Lights 100 (M & NM)
Eve Slim Ultra Lights 100 (M & NM)
Eve Ultra Lights 120 (M & NM)
Falcon Lights 100 (M)
Fiesta–King
Kool Lights 100 (M)
Kool Lights–King (M)
L&M 30's Ultra Lights 100
Malibu Lights 100
More Lights 100 (M & NM)
Parliament Lights–King
Players Lights 25's–King (M & NM)
Pyramid Ultra Lights 100
Salem Lights–King (M)
Savvy Ultra Lights 100
Tareyton Long Lights 100
True 100 (M & NM)
Vantage–King (M & NM)
Virginia Slims Lights 100 (M & NM)
Winston Lights–King

6

0.6 Milligrams Nicotine
Switch next to Box 3

Camel Lights–King
Carlton 120 (M & NM)
Generic Ultra Lights 100 (M & NM)
Generic Ultra Lights–King (M & NM)
Lucky Strike Lights–King
Magna Lites–King
Merit–King (M & NM)
Triumph 100 (M & NM)
Vantage 100 (M & NM)

5

0.5 Milligrams Nicotine
Switch next to Box 3

Benson & Hedges Deluxe Ultra Lights 100
  (M & NM)
Bright 100 (M)
Cambridge Ultra Low Tar 100
Kent III 100
Merit Ultra Lights–King (M & NM)
Merit Ultra Lights 100 (M & NM)
True–King (M & NM)
Vantage Ultra Lights 100
Virginia Slims Ultra Lights 100 (M & NM)
Virginia Super Slims 100 (M & NM)
Winston Ultra Lights–King
Winston Ultra Lights 100

4

0.4 Milligrams Nicotine
Switch next to Box 3

Doral Ultra Lights–King
Doral Ultra Lights 100
Kent III–King
Salem Ultra Lights–King (M)
Salem Ultra Lights 100 (M)
Tareyton Lights–King
Triumph–King (M & NM)
Vantage Ultra Lights–King

3

0.3 Milligrams Nicotine or Less
You're Ready to Quit

Carlton–King (M & NM)
Carlton 100 (M & NM)
Next (in test markets only)
Now–King (M & NM)
Now 100 (M & NM)

Nicorette® (Nicotine Gum)

Nicorette® is a prescription product that can lessen withdrawal symptoms and weight gain after quitting smoking by providing some nicotine through the inside of the cheek. Temporary use of Nicorette is far less dangerous than continuing to smoke. Nicorette provides less nicotine than does cigarette smoking, and it does not have the cancer-causing chemicals in cigarette smoke.

Although Nicorette® is called nicotine "gum," it should be chewed only occasionally to release the nicotine, and then held in a cheek so the nicotine can be absorbed. If Nicorette is chewed rapidly, like regular gum, much of the nicotine is swallowed. Swallowed nicotine does not help relieve withdrawal symptoms, and may cause an upset stomach.

Nicorette® is sold in boxes of ninety-six pieces for about $26-$30 a box. Most former pack-a-day smokers find 12 pieces a day are enough to lessen their withdrawal symptoms; two pack-a-day smokers require about 20 pieces a day. If you use the brand-switching strategy to reduce nicotine intake before quitting, you may need less.

Begin using Nicorette® on your quit date. At the first sign of an urge to smoke, start chewing a piece of Nicorette *very very slowly* until you notice a spicy taste or feel a tingling sensation in your mouth (usually after about 15 chews). Then stop chewing and "park" the Nicorette between your gum and your cheek. After about one minute, when the taste subsides, chew slowly a few times until you taste the Nicorette, and then again hold the piece in your cheek. Each piece is used in this way for about thirty minutes and then discarded.

For maximum effectiveness, avoid consuming any beverage, especially soft drinks, coffee, tea, orange juice, or alcohol for 15 minutes before using Nicorette® (and while the Nicorette is in your mouth). Keep using the Nicorette even if, at first, you don't like the taste. After three months, gradually reduce the number of pieces you use. Many people reduce by one daily piece of Nicorette each week. After you stop using Nicorette, keep a few pieces handy for emergencies.

Nicorette® is not a cure-all. It will help to lessen many withdrawal symptoms but you will still need to continue to use the other coping techniques recommended in this manual.

Be on the lookout for side effects. Chewing Nicorette too fast can produce lightheadedness, nausea, throat and mouth irritation, hiccups, and stomach upset. Other reported side effects include aching in the jaw muscle, headaches, heart palpitations, over-salivation, and sticking to dental work. Report any problems to your doctor.

Nicorette should not be used by women who are pregnant or who may become pregnant while using it, or by people with certain kinds of heart trouble such as severe arrhythmias (irregular heart beats), severe angina (chest pain), or a recent heart attack.

Should You Reduce Caffeine Consumption?

Many people, particularly smokers, consume a lot of caffeine. Caffeine is a stimulant found in coffee, tea, cola, chocolate, and some pain medications. Smokers clear caffeine from their bodies faster than do nonsmokers. That is one reason smokers drink so much coffee and cola.

After you stop smoking, caffeine will stay in your body longer. To offset this, after quitting you should reduce your caffeine consumption by about one third. This apparent reduction is needed to keep the level of caffeine in your body about the same as when you were a smoker. Use the Caffeine Count table on the following pages to plan how you will reduce your caffeine consumption by one third.

Further reductions in caffeine intake may be advisable because caffeine can cause cigarette urges by increasing nervousness, by lowering blood sugar, and through habitual associations with cigarettes:

- **Nervousness.** Caffeine is a stimulant that increases heart rate, nervousness, and blood pressure.

- **Low Blood Sugar.** Caffeine causes blood sugar level (and energy level) to increase and then to fall. Many people experience low blood sugar as a need for a "pick-me-up" — a cigarette, a cup of coffee, or a sugary snack.

- **Habitual Associations.** For most smokers, a cup of coffee and a cigarette go together. After quitting smoking, a cup of coffee may cause urges to smoke because of this habitual link with cigarettes.

Because of the above effects, many stop-smoking programs advise people to stop all caffeine consumption. However, caffeine is addictive. If you abruptly swear off all caffeine, you could suffer withdrawal symptoms such as headaches, irritability, and sleepiness. You don't need these symptoms when you're quitting smoking.

The solution to the caffeine dilemma may be to cut down gradually on caffeine consumption before quitting smoking (in addition to the one-third reduction after quitting). Gradual reductions in caffeine consumption are advisable if you are taking in more than 500 milligrams a day (about five cups of coffee—see the table on the next page), or if you know you are particularly sensitive or reactive to caffeine. To avoid withdrawal symptoms, do not reduce your caffeine consumption by more than 25 percent a week.

To summarize:

1. Before you quit smoking, if you are using a lot of caffeine, you should consider gradually reducing your caffeine consumption.
2. After you quit smoking, reduce permanently your caffeine consumption by one third.

TABLE: The Caffeine Count

Substance	Milligrams of Caffeine
COFFEE, 5 oz.	
Automatic drip	110-150
Percolated	65-125
Instant	40-80
Decaffeinated	1-2
TEA	
Brewed, five minutes (5 oz.)	40-60
Iced, in 12 oz. cans	35-60
SOFT DRINKS, 12 oz.	
Jolt Cola	71
Dr. Pepper	61
Mountain Dew	54
Mello Yello	54
Coca-Cola	50
Pepsi Cola	43
Diet RC Cola	33
Tab	32
Ginger Ale; Fresca	0
Seven Up; Sprite	0
Orange; Root Beer	0
Caffeine Free Colas	0

DRUGS

No Doz — 2 tablets	200
Vivarin — 1 tablet	200
Excedrin — 2 tablets	130
Cafergot — 1 tablet	100
Vanquish — 2 tablets	66
Anacin — 2 tablets	65
Midol — 2 tablets	65
Migrol — 1 tablet	50
Fiorinal — 1 tablet	40
Dristan — 2 tablets	32
Darvon Compound — 1 tablet	32
Coryban-D — 1 tablet	30
Sinarest — 1 tablet	30
Dexatrim*	0
Pamprin	0
Aspirin	0
Tylenol	0
Datril	0
Advil	0
Nuprin	0

CHOCOLATE

Baking chocolate (1 oz.)	35
Chocolate candy bar, small	15-25
Cocoa drink (6 oz.)	5-20

*Dexatrim at one time had caffeine but is now free of caffeine.

Stop the Debate

George succeeded in getting off cigarettes but continued to suffer much longer than most people. Urges were frequent, and with each urge, an internal debate started: "Should I smoke or not? Maybe I could have just one." George was experiencing every withdrawal symptom imaginable. Then something happened to change all that. A smoking friend was diagnosed as having lung cancer. George decided—*really decided*—that he would never smoke again; that he was a permanent nonsmoker no matter what! The withdrawal symptoms disappeared. He suffered no more irritability, no more "nerves," no depression. Why?

Once George really decided that, *no matter what*, he would never smoke again, the internal debate ended. It was his constant debate, the back and forth thoughts about whether or not to have a cigarette, that caused his prolonged suffering.

Once you really decide you are a permanent nonsmoker, urges are irrelevant. You no longer have to think about cigarettes all the time and your mind can go on to more pleasant things.

If you have not yet made a firm decision to quit for good, take some time and think it through one last time. It may not be an easy decision. If, despite mixed feelings, you decide that you want most to quit, make your decision and *do not debate it further*. When you make a firm decision to quit, your new nonsmoking lifestyle will unfold gracefully.

Enlist Allies

Americans pride themselves on being self-reliant, independent, and strong-willed. Consequently, many people try to quit smoking by toughing it out alone, without the support of others. Some people do not even tell others that they are trying to quit. This is not quitting smart. People who actively arrange a support system for their quitting efforts are more likely to succeed, and they succeed with greater comfort.

Ask for the support of several family members and friends. You will want a supportive ally at home, at work, and in social situations. Tell these allies of your plans to quit, ask for their support, and discuss with them specifically *how* they can help you. For example, you might ask them to help by:

- Reading this manual so they understand your quitting program.
- Accompanying you on smoke-free activities (a walk, a movie).
- Helping to talk you through an urge.
- Praising you for not smoking.
- Giving you rewards (a hug, card, flowers).
- Not reminding you of past difficulties in quitting.
- Being tolerant of any negative effects of withdrawal (irritability, nervousness).
- Reminding you that withdrawal symptoms are temporary.

- Not nagging or attempting to police you.
- Pointing out your positive changes (brighter eyes, better smell).
- Expressing confidence in your ability to remain a nonsmoker.
- Realizing that you can use special support for a full year.

Review this list with your allies so you can plan together the best support strategy. Don't be shy about doing this. Your family and friends want you alive and well, and most will be pleased when you request their help.

Be sure to tell all of your allies often how much you appreciate their support. On the three-month anniversary of your quit date, you might send each ally a thank-you note or a small gift.

"Bless Mommy and Daddy, Aunt Emma and Uncle Sid, Cousin Myrna, Dr. Benson and all my support systems."

List the people you will ask to support you:

Supportive person at home

_____

Supportive person at work

_____

Supportive social friend

_____

Note how each ally has agreed to help:

_____

_____

_____

_____

_____

_____

_____

_____

_____

Avoid Smoking Temptations

Before you quit, it's smart to adjust your home, car, and work environments so that they support your quitting. Most important is eliminating or reducing things that serve as triggers for smoking.

Destroy Cigarettes. Just before your quit date, destroy all your cigarettes. The sight and smell of cigarettes will only tempt you. Be sure you search out every last cigarette and cigarette butt and destroy them completely! Also, remove ash trays and lighters.

Avoid Smokers. For your first few weeks as a nonsmoker, avoid being around people who are smoking. Do not schedule lunch dates or social outings with smokers during this vulnerable time. Ask close friends and relatives not to smoke around you.

For the long term, make a point of getting to know your nonsmoking friends better. By spending more time with your nonsmoking friends, you will be more likely to remain a successful long-term nonsmoker.

Avoid Smoky Places. Smoky places tend to serve as triggers for smoking. Try to avoid bars, smoky restaurants, bowling alleys, coffee-break areas, and parties. Even places in your own home or office that you associate with cigarettes, such as your favorite "smoking chair," should be avoided for a time.

Make Cigarette Substitutes Available

Cigarettes occupy your hands, mouth, and mind. They also serve as rewards and as a relief from boredom. Place some of the following substitute items around your house, car, and work area and then use them regularly:

Carry With You / Keep in Your Car
- a pen
- toothpicks or "Stim-u-Dents"
- gum, mints, lollipops
- paper clips to bend
- straws, coffee stirsticks
- hobby items (crossword puzzles)
- a pocket "worry stone" or marbles
- this manual
- a book or magazine
- cinnamon sticks
- dietetic candy*

Keep at home / work
- nuts to crack and eat
- ice to chew on
- carrot/celery sticks
- popcorn (unbuttered)
- flowers to smell and touch
- an enjoyable book
- club soda, water, fruit juice
- walking/running shoes
- raw shelled sunflower seeds
- a toothbrush

*The sweeteners Sorbital and Mannitol, in some sugarless candy and gum, can cause gastric upset and diarrhea when taken in large quantities.

Select Your Quit Date

If you have not already done so, now is the time to select your quit date. This will be your first full day of freedom from cigarettes. Normally, your quit date should be one to three weeks in the future to allow enough time to complete all your important preparations:

– Arranging for the support of family and friends.

– Placing substitutes for cigarettes in your house, car, and workplace.

– If appropriate, completing brand switching and/or discussing Nicorette® with your physician.

– Gradually cutting caffeine consumption, if this is indicated.

– Preparing urge-control strategies by studying the **Quitting** chapter of this manual.

– Destroying all your cigarettes and removing ashtrays (just before your quit date).

If possible, select a quit date that will not be stressful or demanding, perhaps a Saturday or a vacation day. *Write your quit date on the next page* and circle it on your calendar. Stick to your selected date.

**QuitSmart
Quit Contract**

I will quit cold turkey on

_____

and never smoke again.

_____
Signature

_____
Date

QUIT SMART™

CHAPTER II:
Quitting

Hats off to you for getting this far, and for devoting the time and energy to plan ahead for successful quitting. You are now ready for the quitting phase, which begins on your quit date. For some this phase is a period of intense combat with cigarette urges. But you may find that quitting is easier than you expected if you keep withdrawal symptoms in perspective and *actively do things to cope.* In the sections of this chapter, you will learn relaxation methods, various "tricks" that help to control cigarette urges, and how to use your thoughts to make nonsmoking easier.

Continue to use the techniques you have already learned: call on your nonsmoking allies for support and encouragement, use your cigarette substitutes, avoid people who smoke and places where smoking occurs, and refer often to your list of reasons for quitting.

The quitting phase lasts about a week. Then your task increasingly turns from resisting urges to remaining a nonsmoker. This lifetime endeavor involves everything from keeping your emotional balance to dealing with people who try to tempt you to resume smoking. Look ahead at Chapter III, **Remaining a Nonsmoker**, so you will be prepared for this challenge.

Learning To Relax

Most of us suffer to some degree from excess tension and tension-related symptoms such as gastric distress, headaches, insomnia, or pervasive tiredness. Withdrawal from cigarettes may produce a temporary increase in feelings of tension. By practicing the relaxation procedures discussed below, you will learn to relax while keeping your mind clear and sharp.

Taking a Breather. Much of the relaxation attributed to smoking a cigarette is actually due to pausing and taking several slow deep breaths. The smoke drawn in during the breaths does not aid relaxation; nicotine is actually a stimulant. It produces tight muscles and a rise in heart rate and blood pressure. However, pausing to enjoy deep breaths is relaxing, and you will want to maintain that part of the smoking ritual.

Try "taking a breather." Take a slow deep breath, drawing the air deep into your abdomen; hold it a few seconds, and then exhale *slowly* as you let your muscles relax and say to yourself the word "calm" or "relax." Repeat this several times. Practice taking two or three relaxing deep breaths twenty different times a day.

Use daily events as reminders to take breathers. For example, take a breather when you hang up the phone, during television commercials, when you feel annoyed, and whenever you can use a relaxing break. Also, take a breather if you have an urge for a cigarette. The slow deep breaths will leave you more relaxed and in control.

Physical Exercise. Take a daily walk (after dinner is a good time). If you are physically fit and your physician approves, engage in vigorous exercise that you enjoy. Do not rush it, however; progressing too fast in an exercise program can add stress rather than reduce it.

Nutrition. Stress can rob you of vitamins and minerals. If your physician does not object, take a multivitamin supplement.

Sleep. If you have trouble sleeping, be sure you are not drinking a caffeinated beverage within six hours of bedtime. Also, avoid naps. Your sleep should improve within a week or two after quitting. As a nonsmoker, you may require less sleep than you did as a smoker. For example, you might be able to stay up a half hour later before going to bed.

Physical Methods to Relax. Hot baths, massage, stretching exercises, a hot-water bottle, and relaxing music are all calming. Each of these can be used as often as you wish and require no outside help (even massage can be self-massage).

Self-hypnosis. Most people think of hypnosis as one person exerting control over another. Actually, in self-hypnosis a person learns to relax, and then uses that relaxed state to concentrate on suggestions. This person is in control the entire time. Without hypnosis, it is difficult for most people to concentrate well enough to apply the full power of their minds to a single goal.

The QuitSmart Self-Hypnosis Tape teaches relaxation and helps you focus the powers of your mind on remaining comfortably free of cigarettes. See page 87 for more information on self-hypnosis (page 94 provides tape ordering information).

To use the tape, start listening to side one ("Quitting") on your quit date. Listen twice daily during your first week off cigarettes. The next week, listen to side one at least once daily. Thereafter listen to side one or side two ("Remaining a Nonsmoker") as often as needed to remain relaxed and confident of your abilty to steer clear of cigarettes. Do not listen to the tape while driving or operating machinery.

Thinking Makes It So

The human mind has the power to create feelings out of thin air. For example, you may be able to create hunger just by thinking about a juicy steak, or sleepiness by imagining a yawn coming on. This power of the mind can be used in three ways to help you stay free from cigarettes. You can use your thoughts and images to foster a nonsmoking self-image, to control cigarette urges, and to keep life's hassles in perspective.

Foster a nonsmoking self-image. A person's self-image has a powerful effect on behavior. When you think of yourself as a nonsmoker, you will behave as a nonsmoker. You will, for example, view cigarette ads from the critical perspective of a nonsmoker, and you automatically will sit in the nonsmoking section of restaurants. If you feel bored or anxious, you will not interpret those feelings as an urge for a cigarette because nonsmokers do not have such urges.

The effect of self-image on behavior is well known in sports. Greg Louganis became a world champion diver, in part, by thinking of himself as a great diver and by imagining himself performing each dive perfectly. Though not in the same league as Louganis, the author of this manual frequently interrupts poor tennis play by imagining he is Jimmy Conners. As "Jimmy," he is a stronger, more confident player.

You are what you believe. Believing you are a permanent nonsmoker who is calm and happy will naturally lead to that desired outcome. Do not make the mistake of trying to break the cigarette habit while subconsciously thinking of yourself as a smoker. See smoking as something that you did a long time ago; you were a different person then. Now you are a nonsmoker.

Control cigarette urges. Most urges for a cigarette can be controlled by simply focusing your thoughts elsewhere. Focusing your thoughts on an urge to smoke is like focusing on an itchy nose; it will prolong your discomfort. Instead, turn your thoughts to something pleasant and unrelated to smoking, like a walk on the beach.

Keep life's hassles in perspective. You have probably known people who get very upset with the least little mishap, and other people who handle a crisis with aplomb. The ability to "roll with the punches" will be particularly important during your first few weeks without cigarettes. The key to maintaining perspective on life's hassles is the realization that the way you think about a situation will determine your feelings about it. For example, when caught in a traffic jam, you can make yourself very angry by thinking "I'll never be on time; this is awful," or relatively calm by thinking, "This is a chance to 'take a breather' and enjoy the radio."

Your thoughts can make the experience of quitting either difficult or relatively easy. Quitting will be difficult if you tell yourself that withdrawal symptoms are terrible, and that you won't succeed. Instead, tell yourself that any discomfort is tolerable, and that you are adding freedom and self-control to your life. With positive thinking, quitting can be surprisingly easy and fulfilling.

Shakespeare wrote "There is nothing either good or bad, but thinking makes it so." (Hamlet, Act II, Scene 2.) Using your thoughts constructively will help you stay calm during cigarette withdrawal and avoid making "mountains out of molehills."

Keeping Withdrawal Symptoms in Perspective

The initial challenge of breaking the cigarette habit is getting through the physical withdrawal phase. Your body has become accustomed to nicotine in hundreds of daily puffs. The use of brand switching, nicotine gum, or both will lessen any discomfort, but some people may briefly experience some of the following symptoms:

- headaches
- irritability
- muscle aches or cramps
- anxiety
- difficulty sleeping at night
- daytime sleepiness
- craving for tobacco
- lightheadedness
- tingling sensations or numbness in arms and legs
- constipation or diarrhea
- sweating
- coughing
- crying
- difficulty concentrating or remembering things
- increased craving for sweets.

Each person experiences cigarette withdrawal differently. For example, some people feel tense, while others feel drowsy. Many people experience little or no discomfort. Any withdrawal symptoms you may experience are temporary and are a sign that your body is healing itself.

Remember:

1. **Withdrawal symptoms are temporary; they will soon pass.** Symptoms generally peak during the first three to six days and mostly disappear within two to four weeks. Soon after that, as a nonsmoker, you will be healthier and calmer than you were as a smoker.

2. **Urges are short-lived.** It may seem that an urge lasts forever, but actually an urge peaks and subsides within three to five minutes. If you interrupt an urge with a coping technique (deep breaths, pleasant thoughts), you will conquer it even sooner.

3. **Withdrawal symptoms are a sign that your body is healing itself.**

– Tingling sensations in the arms and legs result from improved circulation.

– Lightheadedness may occur as the brain gets more oxygen than it is used to.

– Coughing increases for a few days as the lung's hair-like cilia, no longer paralyzed by tobacco smoke, work overtime to remove tar and debris from the lungs.

– Sweating may increase as chemical substances in tobacco smoke are flushed out of the body through the skin's pores.

4. **Use coping techniques.** Taking deep relaxing breaths, drinking plenty of water, and gradually increasing your daily exercise are a few of the activities that will keep you on top of withdrawal effects.

5. **Notice Positive Changes**. It is important to look for the first signs of physical and mental improvement. After a few days to a week free of cigarettes, you will discover many of the following positive changes:

- You can walk further without feeling winded.
- Your hands and feet are warmer due to improved blood circulation.
- Your complexion is rosier, healthier.
- You breathe more easily with less coughing.
- You have more energy.
- Your sleep improves.
- Your sinuses clear.
- Your teeth and fingers are cleaner.
- Your resting pulse rate drops as your heart's job becomes easier.
- Your senses of smell, taste, and hearing improve.
- You have a sense of rebirth and pride in your accomplishment.

After being free of cigarettes for several days, begin keeping a running list of the positive changes you are experiencing.

_____

_____

_____

_____

_____

_____

_____

_____

_____

_____

_____

_____

_____

_____

_____

Habit Buster Tips

The smoking habit may be strong, but it is also dumb—you can outsmart it. Small changes in those parts of your daily routine that are associated with cigarettes can so confuse your smoking habit that you will emerge victorious. Try the following:

– **Leave the table as soon as you finish eating.** Brush your teeth or take a walk. This will disrupt the association of finishing a meal and having a cigarette.

– **Change habits that you associate with smoking.** If you generally smoked while talking on the phone, talk in a different room, hold the phone in the other hand, or sit in a different chair. If you usually smoked while sitting in your favorite chair, avoid that "smoking" chair for a while. Similarly, if possible, sit in the non-smoking areas of restaurants and planes, and avoid for a while friends who smoke.

– **Keep busy.** Take up a hobby, go to the movies, go for a walk, work around the house, call or visit friends, or write letters.

– **Increase your physical activity.** Exercise stimulates many of the same physical responses as nicotine, but in a positive way. It also rejuvenates your blood's supply of oxygen and releases mood-elevating chemicals to the brain. Walk daily, exercise, or take up a sport you enjoy. The next time you need a pick-me-up, try some jumping jacks or a walk in the fresh air.

- **Keep your hands occupied.** Substitute a paper clip, rubber band, coin, stone, or pen.
- **Keep oral substitutes close by.** Use sugarless mints or gum, straws, toothpicks, cinnamon sticks, carrot and celery sticks, crushed ice and water.

Coping Techniques To Remember

1. **Drink plenty of fluids**. Drink lots of water and other beverages (at least eight glasses a day) to help flush the cigarette poisons from your body.

2. **Avoid swings in blood sugar**. Eat regular meals rich in protein and complex carbohydrates (fruits, vegetables, grains) and limit sugar and sugar-containing foods.

3. **Relax**. Perform your "take a breather" ritual many times a day and whenever you experience a strong urge to smoke.

4. **Remind yourself often that urges are temporary**. An urge passes within three to five minutes—you can wait it out.

5. **Think about what you will buy**. Plan how you will spend the money no longer wasted on cigarettes and medical bills.

6. **Ask friends and relatives for help**. Tell them you are quitting and how they can help.

7. **Praise yourself**. Think often of your pride at resisting cigarettes. Mentally pat yourself on the back each time you outsmart an urge.

8. **Note your improvements**. For example, if your sense of smell has improved or you have more "wind," actively focus your thoughts on these positive changes.

9. **Express your frustrations and anger**. Gently stick up for your rights, or pound a pillow, or take a walk. Do something with your frustrations; don't let them do something to you by serving as an excuse for a cigarette.

10. **Call Washington, D.C. for friendly advice.** Dial 1-202-682-3733 for a different recorded message every day.

11. **Feel proud.** When you see someone smoking, feel proud that you no longer engage in such a silly, harmful habit. Let yourself feel a bit superior and smug.

QUIT SMART ™

CHAPTER III:
Remaining a Nonsmoker

Congratulations! You are over the worst. From here on, urges become less frequent. Your task now turns increasingly to remaining a nonsmoker over the long haul. This chapter will prepare you to overcome situations that often induce new exsmokers to "fall off the wagon."

Relapse is most common during periods of negative emotions (anger, frustration, anxiety, or depression). To keep your mood on an even keel, you will learn to increase self-rewards and decrease hassles. Continued use of your relaxation skills ("taking a breather," daily exercise) will also help control negative emotions.

Relapse occurs for some people when they encounter pressure from others to "have just one." You will learn firm rebuttals to such smoking come-ons. Likewise, from time to time your own thoughts may tempt you ("I need a cigarette to handle this crisis") and firm responses are necessary here, too. You will also learn the folly of thinking you can smoke "just one."

Finally, weight gain, which may or may not be due to quitting smoking, often serves as an excuse for relapse. Instead, you will learn to control your weight by using techniques similar to those you used to conquer the smoking habit.

Maintaining Your Emotional Balance

Each of us maintains our emotional balance by making sure our daily lives include enough pleasures to offset life's hassles. Life's hassles include too much work to be done, unpleasant obligations, and unappreciative people. Life's pleasures include a hug from a child, a thank you from a friend, doing things you want to do, pleasant thoughts, or buying things you want. If you have too many hassles and not enough pleasures, your life falls out of balance, causing you to get frustrated, angry and depressed.

Smoking was mostly a pleasurable activity for you. Therefore, having decided to get free of cigarettes, it is wise to maintain your balance by increasing other pleasures in your life and by decreasing hassles. By doing so, you can minimize the sadness that often occurs two or three weeks after quitting. Many new exsmokers fail to act on these ideas because they have trouble being nice to themselves; but so much depends on maintaining your emotional balance—your happiness, your productivity, the happiness of those around you. Get some ideas from the following lists of ways other exsmokers kept their emotional balance.

Accentuate the Positive

- Jennifer bought a flower for her desk each week.
- Rod bought a new cassette tape every week.
- Bob told himself often how proud he was to be off cigarettes.

- Whenever Julie saw a cigarette machine, she mentally patted herself on the back for saving so much money by not smoking.
- Sue treated herself to some costume jewelry.
- Karen took pleasant walks after dinner.
- Jill allowed herself a bubble bath.
- Jack started getting a massage each week.
- Alice joined a health spa and enjoyed attending several times a week.
- Steve remembered to pause for slow relaxing deep breaths.
- Sam allowed himself to sleep late on Saturday mornings.

Eliminate the Negative

- Mary resigned from an unpleasant committee that she had felt obligated to attend.
- Elaine eliminated the hassle of phone calls interrupting the family dinner by taking the phone off the hook.
- Sam decided to stop feeling guilty for wanting some time to himself.
- Ron traded his least favorite chore—loading the dishwasher—for walking the dog, a pleasant way of increasing exercise.
- Jackie discussed with her husband the need for a more equitable distribution of household duties.

List the positives you plan to accentuate:

_____

_____

_____

_____

_____

_____

_____

_____

_____

_____

_____

_____

_____

List the negatives you plan to eliminate:

_____

_____

_____

_____

_____

_____

Rebuffing Smoking Come-ons

Most people will try to help you stay free of cigarettes, but some may actually try to tempt you to smoke again. This can happen because your success threatens them or because they are impatient with your temporary irritability or other withdrawal symptoms. Either way, it pays to prepare yourself to stand up for your decision to remain a nonsmoker.

Smoking Come-on	Possible Response
"Have a cigarette, just one won't hurt."	"No, it's stupid to tempt fate. I'm glad to be a nonsmoker."
"You're so irritable; have a cigarette."	"I may be irritable, but I'm not crazy. Please don't offer me a cigarette."
"We're having such a good time; join me in a cigarette."	"I don't smoke anymore. Why don't you join me in a walk?"
"Congratulations on a good job. You deserve a cigarette."	"I don't smoke, but I'll have a soft drink."
"Have a cigarette; you're going to die sooner or later anyway."	"No thanks, I'd prefer later."

SMOKING COME-ONS...

Controlling the Enemy Within

As you reviewed the smoking come-ons, you may have realized that you have used some of these come-ons against yourself. Perhaps you told yourself "have just one" or "have a cigarette to calm your irritability" or "you deserve a cigarette." When this happens, it pays to be just as forceful with yourself as you will be if somebody else goes against your decision to be free of cigarettes. Look back over the come-ons on the preceding pages and put a check mark by any that you have used on yourself in the past.

Listed below are other common self-generated come-ons and possible rebuttals.

Self Come-On	Rebuttal
Nostalgia: "Smoking was so great with coffee."	"Maybe, maybe not, but I also remember times it tasted bad and made me feel sick."
Crisis: "I can't handle this without a cigarette."	"No, a cigarette only makes me feel more defeated. I'll take a few deep breaths and handle this."
Anger: "I'll show that so-and-so; I'll smoke a cigarette."	"I'll stick up for myself *and* stick by *my* decision to be a nonsmoker."
Defeatism: "Since I'm a jerk anyway, I may as well smoke."	"Nobody's perfect, but I'm proud that I quit smoking."

Staying On the Wagon

Did you know that among exsmokers who have "just one" cigarette, three out of four soon return to regular smoking? After two cigarettes, nine out of ten exsmokers return to regular smoking. Some exsmokers think they can beat the odds—but why try? Other exsmokers want to smoke "just one" to prove how strong they are. However, it shows more strength to resist temptation.

When an exsmoker has one cigarette, guilt and discouragement set in and the label of "smoker" is assumed again. Believing that the battle is already lost and perceiving smoking as a pleasurable consolation, the exsmoker resumes regular smoking ("I already blew it, so I might as well smoke another.")

You have made a wise decision to quit smoking and have invested considerable time and energy into becoming a nonsmoker. It only makes sense now to protect your investment by *never allowing yourself "just one."* Underscore your determination to stay completely free of cigarettes by signing the contract below. Ask one of your allies to witness your pledge.

 QUIT SMART

**QuitSmart
No Smoke Contract**

I have considered the pros and cons, and have decided to remain totally free of cigarettes. I hereby pledge to continue to use all my efforts to keep cigarettes permanently out of my life.

_____
Your Signature

_____
Witness

_____
Date

Systematic Weight Control

Weight gain is a prime reason some people give for resuming smoking. About one out of two people who quit smoking gains weight. If you are in this group, realize that the extra pounds are likely to be temporary, and devise a systematic weight control strategy.

Avoid starvation diets, fad diets, and diet pills. Eat three nutritious meals a day while limiting fattening foods. Use a non-caloric sweetener. It is a good idea, however, to allow for an occasional snack or sweet by cutting back calories elsewhere. If you entirely forbid certain foods that you desire, these foods can become so tempting that it is only a matter of time before you give up your diet.

Set realistic weight-loss goals. Look for gradual reductions in weight, generally not exceeding one to two pounds a week.

Controlling weight has many similarities to controlling smoking. Many of the methods that you have found helpful in maintaining freedom from cigarettes can be equally effective in controlling overeating:

- **Use your stress-management skills**. When tempted to break your diet, "take a breather" to relax and control the urge to overeat.
- **Engage in regular physical exercise**. Regular exercise is the single most important factor in sustained weight control. A daily walk reduces stress, lessens hunger, and burns calories.

- **Avoid overeating temptations**. Eliminate things which trigger you to eat fattening foods. The best way to do this is to have no fattening foods in the house. Grocery shop only when you are not hungry, and avoid desserts and fattening foods in favor of low-fat munchies (celery, carrot sticks, sugarless candy and gum).

- **Think of yourself as a healthy eater.** Remember "thinking makes it so." Think of yourself as a person who is very selective about what s/he eats. See yourself as a person who cultivates a slow "picky" eating style, and always leave some food on your plate. You may lose your membership in the "clean plate club," but "thinking thin" is the easiest way to change your weight permanently.

- **Enlist allies**. Tell selected friends and family members that you are going to lose weight and ask for their help. Specify exactly what you want them to do (or stop doing).

- **Control the enemy within.** The same types of tempting thoughts that you have overcome to stay a nonsmoker will need to be overcome to maintain your desired weight. Look back at the section titled "Controlling the Enemy Within" and plan how you will rebuff tempting thoughts arising in situations of nostalgia, crisis, anger, and defeatism.

- **Consider using Nicorette.®** New exsmokers who use Nicorette gain only half as much weight as new exsmokers who don't use Nicorette.
- **Use self-rewards.** When you succeed at eating sensibly, reward yourself. Avoid depression and anger by increasing the pleasures in your life and decreasing the hassles or negatives. This is particularly essential if you are watching your weight at the same time that you are breaking the cigarette habit.
- **Listen to your self-hypnosis tape.** Both sides of the tape help you maintain your desired weight by fostering relaxation and an attitude of caring for your body. Side one of the tape includes specific hypnotic suggestions to help you avoid unwanted weight gain.

If you find yourself faced with a weight gain, avoid the temptation to resume smoking. Sadly, most people who go back to cigarettes "because of weight gain" do not then lose the weight. Cigarettes are not a treatment for weight gain. So, if you put on weight, use your head—"LoseSmart" by systematically tackling that problem much as you systematically overcame smoking.

Dangers of Smoking / Benefits of Nonsmoking

Often smokers avoid learning all the harmful effects of cigarettes because these effects are so frightening. Likewise, smokers may see little point in dwelling on the benefits of nonsmoking that they are missing. However, now that you are free of cigarettes, knowing the dangers of smoking and benefits of quitting will strengthen your resolve to remain a permanent nonsmoker.

Physical Problems of Smokers

- Heart disease
- Lung cancer
- Emphysema and bronchitis
- Stomach ulcers
- Cancers of the mouth, larynx, esophagus, bladder, kidney, pancreas, stomach, and reproductive organs
- Bone calcium loss (osteoporosis) and tooth loss
- Facial wrinkles (due to poor circulation, smoke, and puckering)
- Confusion and poor memory (due to low blood oxygen levels)
- Stroke (due to hardening or clogging of blood vessels in the brain)
- Hearing loss (due to poor circulation in the inner ear)
- Poor night vision
- Headaches

- Reproductive organ malfunctions: decreased sexual drive, decreased fertility, early female menopause, increased odds of miscarriage and birth defects (from defective sperm caused by *father's* smoking), and low birth weight in infants born to smoking mothers.
- Back problems (due to decreased circulation to spinal disks, decreased elasticity of tendons and ligaments, and back wrenching coughs)
- Sleep difficulty (due to the stimulant effects of nicotine)
- Shortness of breath
- Colds, coughs, and sore throats. Smokers suffer from twice the respiratory illness of nonsmokers and each illness persists longer.

Some of the 4000 Chemicals Smokers Inhale:

Acetaldehyde, acetone, aceturitrile, acrolein, acrylonitrile, ammonia, arsenic, benzene, butylamine, carbon monoxide, carbon dioxide, cresols, crotononitrile, DDT, dimethylamine, endrin, ethylamine, formaldehyde, furfural hydroquinone, hydrogen cyanide (used in the gas chamber), hydrogen sulfide, methacrolein, methyl alcohol, methylamine, nickel compounds, nicotine, nitric oxide, nitrogen dioxide, phenol, polonium-210 (radioactive), pyridine, "tar" (burned plant resins), 2-3 butadione.

Exsmoker Advantages to Keep in Mind

You will save money—lots of money. Assuming cigarettes cost $1.25 a pack, if you were a two-pack-a-day smoker, you will save $912 a year just by not smoking cigarettes—that's $18,240 in twenty years! By putting the $912 each year into a retirement account earning 10% interest, after twenty years you will have over $52,000, and after thirty years you will have over $150,000!

An exsmoker also saves money by being much less likely than a smoker to suffer a serious illness. On average, a forty-four-year-old man who quit a two-pack-a-day habit will save $34,000 in medical costs, and in earnings and productivity not lost due to illness.* Added to the retirement account discussed above, this man would enjoy an extra $86,000 to $184,000.

You may also be able to save money on your insurance premiums. Reduced rates are offered by some companies to nonsmokers and exsmokers on insurance for health, life, car, and house. Smokers pay higher house insurance premiums because they tend to burn their houses down. Higher car insurance for smokers is because they have more accidents, perhaps due to fumbling for cigarettes rather than watching the road.

* Oster, G., Colditz, G., and Kelly, N.L. The Economic Costs of Smoking and Benefits of Quitting. *World Smoking and Health*, Summer 1984, pp. 9-16.

People close to you will be healthier. Children whose mothers smoke have increased risks of colds, bronchitis, and pneumonia. The nonsmoking spouse of a heavy smoker may have increased risk of lung cancer.

You feel better. You have more energy, you look better (more bright-eyed), your heart rate is lower, your hands and feet are warmer due to improved circulation, and you are justifiably proud of getting free of cigarettes. Listed below are benefits noted by exsmokers just a few weeks after breaking their cigarette habits. How many of these benefits are you enjoying?

- I feel in control of my fate for the first time in fifteen years.
- I like not burning holes in my clothes and furniture.
- I've inspired others to quit.
- I don't believe how calm I am.
- I feel more poised in social situations.
- Proud that I don't need a social "crutch" anymore.
- Now I can present a good model to my kids.
- Glad to know that past failures were due to lack of knowledge rather than lack of willpower.
- I feel great!
- I have so much more time.
- It's amazing how much I get done now that I have two hands.
- I enjoy having more money to spend on me.

- No more sinus headaches—it's wonderful.
- My skin is healthy pink instead of ash gray.
- Sour stomach is completely gone.
- Now I can play two sets of tennis without fading from lack of lung power.
- The house is cleaner, and smells fresher.
- My sex drive picked up; I feel ten years younger.
- I eat slower and enjoy my food—don't rush through the meal to get a cigarette.
- I enjoyed the halftime show at a basketball game while the addicts rushed out for a cigarette.
- I feel more attractive—actually, I *am* more attractive.
- I no longer hide my anger in a cloud of smoke.
- I feel self-confident.
- I'm starting to take better care of myself in other ways.
- I don't have to empty dirty ashtrays ever again.
- I no longer have to feel embarrassed about being a smoker.
- I can feel smug when I see tobacco ads.
- No more tobacco film on my car windows.
- I'm keeping things in better perspective; I now see little hassles as *little* hassles.
- I no longer have to make excuses about why I'm still smoking.
- Went through a two-hour movie with no desire to smoke.

- No more angry looks from people whose air is being polluted.
- At the airport, loved being able to say "non-smoking section, please."
- Proud that I quit just for me.
- It's great not to worry about starting an accidental fire.
- I don't have to worry about my smoke hurting others.
- I sleep better and wake up feeling refreshed.
- My heart stopped skipping beats all the time.
- My lover tells me I'm more "kissable."
- I climbed the stairs to the third floor and could still talk.
- I feel so strong and competent.
- My husband told me he liked my new perfume—the same one I generally wear but without the smoke smell.
- I love smelling flowers now.
- I'm the envy of the office—they all want to quit now.
- I no longer feel like a social outcast.
- I got my teeth cleaned and they stayed clean.
- I smile more.
- Don't have to worry about always having available a cigarette, lighter, and ashtray.
- I love saying, "I'm a nonsmoker."
- I seem to have more time to enjoy myself.
- I haven't had a cold in months.

- That hacking smoker's cough is gone—now I breathe easy.
- My hair no longer smells like stale smoke.
- I look forward to living a longer healthier life.
- I don't need as much sleep as I used to.
- I feel good about taking better care of my body.
- I no longer worry about a heart attack.
- I feel more sexually attractive.
- I enjoy being the resident expert at work on how to quit smoking.
- Nasal passages are clear—I can breathe.
- The pain in my chest is gone.
- No longer feel tired when I get up.
- No longer cough up black stuff.
- I don't believe how calm I feel.
- My hands are steadier.
- My ulcer calmed down.
- I don't have to hide behind a cigarette anymore.
- I can be close to people without worrying about smoker's breath.
- No longer have to frantically read the signs to see if it's O.K. to smoke.
- New man I met told me he would never date a smoker.
- Glad I "QuitSmart" instead of gritting my teeth and suffering.
- I'm so proud.

What Next?

Continue to use your coping techniques. Urges will arise less and less frequently, but when they do come, they may still be quite strong.

> **List the coping techniques you have found most helpful and will continue to use.**
>
> _____
>
> _____
>
> _____
>
> _____
>
> _____

Remember to be extra nice to yourself. To prevent post-quitting blues, or to overcome them if they occur, be extra nice to yourself—do things *you* want to do. Use the money you are saving by not smoking to buy luxuries you will enjoy. After the initial challenge and excitement of quitting, maintaining nonsmoking can seem anticlimactic. People around you may be less supportive, thinking you already have it made. Consequently, it is up to you to pamper yourself over the next several months.

Review this manual periodically. After being free of cigarettes for a few weeks, there is a tendency to stop doing the things that helped you quit successfully. Keep this manual close by and reread selected sections to maintain your nonsmoking skills. Continue to write in the manual to keep it current. After this section, space is provided for notes. Jot down the techniques you plan to use to deal with a problem situation. Note your improvements since quitting, or just write your impressions of the process of maintaining freedom from cigarettes.

What if you slip and have a cigarette? If this were to happen, you would need to perform some strenuous mental calisthenics to have a chance of climbing back on the wagon. You would probably feel guilty or weak-willed and label yourself "a smoker." Since "thinking makes it so," the temptation to smoke another cigarette would be very strong.

Treat any cigarette as a single isolated incident and continue to think of yourself as a nonsmoker. Analyze what situation led to the cigarette and plan how to handle that situation next time. Then, review your list of reasons for quitting and renew your resolve to remain totally free of cigarettes.

Quit Clinics can help. For many, the support and encouragement provided by a formal quit-smoking clinic is invaluable. If you are having more difficulty remaining free of cigarettes than you would like, consider attending a clinic. To locate clinics in your area, call your physician, the local American Cancer Society or American Lung Association, or Psychology/Psychiatry Departments of local colleges and hospitals. It takes experience to become skilled in helping people quit smoking, so steer away from clinics or clinic leaders who have a short history. Also, be skeptical of programs which claim long-term (six months to one year) success rates of 60 percent or more. A 50 percent success rate would be exceptionally good.

Plan an anniversary celebration. For your six-month anniversary of freedom from cigarettes, do something special. Use the hundreds of dollars that did not go up in smoke to have a party, to take a trip, or to purchase something special just for you.

My six-month anniversary of freedom from smoking is

_____
(date)

To celebrate I will:

_____

_____

_____

_____

_____

_____

Help others. Your success may inspire others to quit. You can help them by sharing your knowledge of the quitting process, and by being a supportive ally. Your physician, dentist, and company health nurse will be interested in knowing about your experience with the QuitSmart method. They want to help people quit—they see the illness and death caused by cigarettes every day. They may want to write the publisher for information about training seminars and materials available to help them in counseling smokers to "QuitSmart."

You have accomplished much in reading this manual. The experience of considering how your behavior affects your health in this one area of smoking may start you toward a healthier lifestyle in other areas. The routine wearing of seat belts, good nutritional practices, and a prudent exercise program soon become a part of many exsmokers' lives. Be good to yourself and enjoy your new lifestyle.

Notes

Appendix: Self-Hypnosis

The QuitSmart Self-Hypnosis cassette tape is recommended to augment the skills you have learned from this manual. The tape will help you relax and apply the full power of your mind to becoming and remaining a comfortable nonsmoker.

Hypnosis is not the magical state that you may have heard. You undoubtedly have experienced hypnosis when you become absorbed in a movie, a book, or a musical passage. When you become absorbed in one thing, you are less distracted by your thoughts or your surroundings.

The self-hypnosis tape features the deep melodic voice of Robert Conroy to help you relax and concentrate on the helpful suggestions.

Side One of the tape, **Quitting**, eases you through your first few weeks without cigarettes. Suggestions are given to help you relax and enjoy healthy alternatives to smoking, as you avoid unwanted weight gain or other negative side effects.

Side Two, **Remaining a Nonsmoker**, helps to instill the attitude of inner calm, strength, and contentment that is most helpful in staying free of cigarettes for a lifetime.

Listening to either side of the tape requires less than 15 minutes. Instructions on tape use are provided in the "Questions and Answers" section that follows. Ordering information appears on the last page of this manual.

HYPNOSIS: QUESTIONS AND ANSWERS

What is hypnosis?
Hypnosis is relaxation with focused attention. You have probably experienced hypnosis while watching an engaging movie or listening to music. Whenever you relax and become so focused on one thing that you are not easily distracted, you are using the powerful state of mind called hypnosis.

How should I use the self-hypnosis tape?
Pick a time and place where you won't be disturbed for at least 15 minute. Turn the lights down, get comfortable in a chair, sofa, or bed that supports all parts of your body. Start the tape and relax.

How often should I listen to the tape?
Hypnosis works by repetition. The more times you listen to the tape, the better. Try to listen to the tape twice a day during your first week of freedom from cigarettes, and once a day thereafter for as long as you need or want to continue. Some good times to listen are early morning and late afternoon.

How will I know if I was in a hypnotic state?
You will simply feel relaxed, your hands may feel heavy and warm, and they may tingle. You may also notice some time distortion, with the tape

seeming to play for more or less time than it actually requires. In any case, you do not need to be in a deeply hypnotized state to benefit from the tape.

Which side of the tape should I listen to?
Start listening to side one of the tape ("Quitting") on your quit date. Listen twice daily during your first week off cigarettes. The next week, listen to side one once daily and begin listening to side two ("Remaining a Nonsmoker"). Thereafter, listen to side one or two as often as you want or need to, emphasizing the side you find most relaxing and helpful.

Should I concentrate hard and try to remember everything on the tape?
No. Just relax and let the tape "be there" without trying to concentrate on every word. Listen to the voice but don't worry about the words too much.

What if I get stuck in hypnosis and can't get out?
The hypnotic state is between sleep and wakefulness, you pass through this state whenever you fall asleep and again when you wake up. If you are tired when you listen to the tape, you could fall asleep. You would awaken as you normally do—when you are rested, or when there is a noise or someone calls your name.

Can I use the tape at night to help me fall asleep?
Yes, but the suggestions on the tape are most helpful if you are in the hypnotic state between sleep and wakefulness. Therefore, it is best to listen to the tape and then allow yourself to go to sleep. The instructions at the end of side two may help—they tell you to return to your normal waking state, "unless you have decided to use this tape to fall asleep."

Is it o.k. to listen to the tape while driving?
No. Since hypnosis causes drowsiness, **do not listen while driving** or operating machinery.

Will the tape benefit me in any way in addition to helping me break free from cigarettes?
It will help you to relax more quickly and completely. This can reduce the frequency of stress symptoms such as headaches, upset stomach, irritability, and sleep difficulties.

Order Form

Please send me the following:

____ **QuitSmart: A Guide to Freedom
from Cigarettes** ($6.95 each)   _____

____ **QuitSmart Self-Hypnosis
Audiotape** ($9.95 each)   _____

____ **QuitSmart Kit** — manual and tape
ordered as a set ($14.95 each)   _____

____ **The Health Professional's Guide to
Helping Patients QuitSmart**
($2.00 each)   _____

____ **QuitSmart Lapel Pin** ($2.95 each)   _____

North Carolinians add 5% sales tax.   _____

Shipping: add $3.00 for the first item,
plus 50¢ for each additional item. (We
ship UPS or first class U.S. Mail.)   _____

Total enclosed   _____

I understand that I may return any item within 30
days for a full refund if not satisfied.

Name _____

Address _____

City _____

State _____   Zip _____

Send order to: **JB Press, Department B
P.O. Box 4843, Duke Station
Durham, NC 27706**

☐ Please send information on quantity discounts.

☐ Please send information on QuitSmart training
seminars and materials for health professionals.

Order Form

Please send me the following:

_____ **QuitSmart: A Guide to Freedom from Cigarettes** ($6.95 each)   _____

_____ **QuitSmart Self-Hypnosis Audiotape** ($9.95 each)   _____

_____ **QuitSmart Kit** — manual and tape ordered as a set ($14.95 each)   _____

_____ **The Health Professional's Guide to Helping Patients QuitSmart** ($2.00 each)   _____

_____ **QuitSmart Lapel Pin** ($2.95 each)   _____

North Carolinians add 5% sales tax.   _____

Shipping: add $3.00 for the first item, plus 50¢ for each additional item. (We ship UPS or first class U.S. Mail.)   _____

Total enclosed   _____

I understand that I may return any item within 30 days for a full refund if not satisfied.

Name _____

Address _____

City _____

State _____   Zip _____

Send order to: **JB Press, Department B**
P.O. Box 4843, Duke Station
Durham, NC 27706

☐ Please send information on quantity discounts.

☐ Please send information on QuitSmart training seminars and materials for health professionals.